# OH!
## THAT'S FUNNY!
# 101
# HILARIOUS
# OHIO
# JOKES

*by* **MARJORIE J. PRESTON
& FRIENDS**

**OH! That's Funny! 101 Hilarious Ohio Jokes**

Printed at Outlandish Press in Cleveland, Ohio

First Printing, November 2020

ISBN: 978-1-948554-20-6

Library of Congress Control Number: 2020922015

*In Memory of*
*Andy Craze, Mark Rapp and Norman Tischler*

## Author's Note

This book was begun during a snowstorm at the end of 2012 and finished during another snowstorm at the beginning of 2013. Thank goodness the power held. I continued edits on it in 2015 and during the pandemic in 2020. It's a testament to the spirit of the people of Ohio that we stay year after year despite those pesky seasons, and a testament to my stubbornness that the book was finished.

Friends have submitted some of their favorite jokes, and though they may not have written the jokes themselves, the person credited is the one who told me the joke. If you see my name next to a joke, it might be one I wrote, changed slightly or just overheard somewhere. Sometimes I like the punchline but not the setup of a joke, so I'll change it around and leave the punchline the same. Sometimes a joke about another state or city works well with an Ohio reference, too, and I've done that occasionally here.

I grew up in Bowling Green, so there may be a few jokes about my hometown, or a few jabs at BGSU's rival, University of Toledo. It's just too easy to make fun of an area you've lived in for twenty years. Now that I'm back in Ohio (after eight years in NYC), my family has settled in Cleveland. You will indeed find some Cleveland Browns jokes. We tell jokes in Cleveland to stay warm, if nothing else.

One section is full of "You Might Live in Ohio if..." jokes, and I've received those jokes from many sources, but would specifically like to thank David Lenahan, Hal Dendurent, and Tara Wilcoxon for compiling these jokes. The list I created is a mish-mash of these "You Know You're From Ohio When..."- type lists we get from our friends.

You'll find old gems and new twists on old themes, plays on words and local Ohio color. There's something for everyone in this book. Many thanks to Kyle J. Osborne at Outlandish Press for publishing the book, and designer Michelle Dimuzio for her work on the colorful cover – and for hanging in there with me for two years after I first asked for her help. Thanks to my marketing pro friend Jeff Rutherford for the idea for the book, and to my author friends Shannon Okey, Dave Schwensen and Michelle Vancisin for invaluable advice along the way. Enjoy!

– Marjorie J. Preston

1) What's round on the ends and high in the middle?

O-HI-O.

– Marni Zollinger

2) Q: What do you call forty-seven millionaires around a TV watching the Super Bowl?

A: The Cleveland Browns.

– Meagen Howe

3) A man walks into a bar in Cleveland with a duck under his arm. The duck is quacking loudly. The bartender says, "Hey, if you can't keep that duck quiet, you're going to have to leave." The owner of the duck says, "Oh, he won't be any problem," so the bartender lets them stay. The Browns game is on and every time the Browns score a field goal, the duck waddles up and down the bar, quacking. The bartender says, "Hey, tell that duck to settle down," and surely enough the duck settles down, until the next time the Browns kick a field goal. The duck again waddles up and down the bar, quacking. The bartender asks the man, "What does he do when we make a touchdown?" The owner of the duck says, "I have no idea."

– Andrew Craze

4) Q: What happened to Dorothy Fuldheim?

A: Dick Goddard.

– Lynn M. Hones

5) A city lady and her friend were driving through rural Ohio when she saw some cows. "What a cute bunch of cows!" said the city lady. "Not a bunch, herd," said her friend, correcting her. "Heard of what?" asked the city lady. "Herd of cows," said her friend. "Of course I've heard of cows!" said the city lady. "No, a cow herd," said her friend. The city lady responded, "What do I care if a cow heard? I have no secrets to keep from a cow!"

– Marjorie J. Preston

6) Four friends head out to a cow pasture in central Ohio to see if they can tip a cow. Unfortunately, they sneak up to a bull and try to tip him. At first the strong, heavy animal just stands there, barely moving while the group tries unsuccessfully to tip him. Then, he turns and chases the group away. Walking back toward the other cows, the bull says to the cows, "Can you believe these guys thought they could just come and tip me over?" The other cows say, "Don't they know you can't just tip over a bull? And the bull says, "That's right, we bulls wobble, but we don't fall down."

– Marjorie J. Preston

7) There was once a man from Ohio with two wives: a pretty wife, Sandra, and an ugly wife, Bula. He always slept with his Ashtabula.

– Meagen Howe

8) Q: What do you call a corned beef sandwich that the server drops just before serving it to you?

A: An Earnest Byner.

– James Lenahan

9) The safest place to be in a tornado is the endzone at Browns Stadium, because there are no touchdowns there.

– Darcy Lindner

10) Why doesn't Columbus have a professional sports team? Because then Cleveland and Cincinnati would want one.

– James Lenahan and Kate Kikel

11) What's the difference between a baby and a Clevelander?
The baby will eventually stop whining.

– Thomas Mulready

12) Two hunters in Coshocton, Ohio are walking together when they spot tracks in the snow. The first hunter says, "Those must be boar tracks." The second hunter replies, "Oh, no, those are definitely deer tracks." And that was when the train hit them.

– Marjorie J. Preston and her dad, Jerry Milnor

13) There are four seasons in Ohio: winter, more winter, still winter and road construction.

– Max Beckett

14) Q: What is Ohio's state flower?

A: Orange construction barrels.  They pop up in the spring
and only fade away when the snow flies.

– Betty Winslow

15) Why do the trees in Ohio lean to the East?  Because Michigan blows and Pittsburgh sucks.

– Judi Strauss

16) As a trucker stops for a red light, a blonde catches up. She jumps out of her car, runs up to his truck, and knocks on the door.

The trucker lowers the window, and she says, "Hi, my name is Rachel, and you are losing some of your load."
The trucker ignores her and proceeds down the street. When the truck stops for another red light, the girl catches up again. She jumps out of her car, runs up and knocks on the door. Again, the trucker lowers the window.

As if they've never spoken, the blonde says brightly, "Hi, my name is Rachel, and you are losing some of your load!"

Shaking his head, the trucker ignores her again and continues down the street. At the third red light, the same thing happens again. All out of breath, the blonde gets out of her car, runs up, knocks on the truck door. The trucker rolls down the window.
Again she says, "Hi, my name is Rachel, and you are losing some of your load!"

When the light turns green the trucker revs up and races to the next light. When he stops this time, he hurriedly gets out of the truck, and runs back to the blonde.

He knocks on her window, and after she lowers it, he says, "Hi, my name is Mark, it's winter in Ohio and I'm driving the SALT TRUCK!"

– Ali Gottfried

17) Q: What's the only thing that grows in Toledo?

A: The crime rate.

– Maryanne Spielman

18) Tontogany, Ohio: like Bowling Green but without all the glitz and glitter.

– Dwight Miller

19) Q: Do you know where Engagement, Ohio is?

A: Between Dayton and Marion.

– Karen Adams

20) Flush your toilet twice, the advice goes.  Pemberville needs the water!

– Keith Schauweker

21) (In the 60s, a burglar was arrested in Bowling Green for impersonating an officer. The joke at the time went like this:)

If you hear a burglar in your basement, go down and get his badge number.

– Dan Horner

22) Driving through Bowling Green, I realized parts of it smell like poo.  At first I blamed the baby, but then I realized it was just Poe Ditch.

– Lorian Jenkins and Marjorie J. Preston

23) The trouble with the Buckeyes football team, just like the poisonous nut, is they're not usually under enough heat to be of any use.

– Marjorie J. Preston

24) Q: What's the capital of Ohio?

A: Capital O, of course.

– Marjorie J. Preston

25) Q: What's the capital of West Virginia?

A: Akron.

– Eric Preston

26) A man in his late seventies comes home from playing a round of golf at Big Met Golf Course in Fairview Park, Ohio.

He throws down his clubs and declares, "I'm through with golf!"

His wife says, "Why? You love the game."

He says, "Yeah I do, but I can't see where the ball goes anymore."

She says, "Take your cousin Marty. He sees great."
He says, "Marty is 86."

She says, "Marty sees perfectly and he doesn't get out much."

So the next day the man and Marty are on the course and he says, "OK, Marty. Are you watching?"

Marty says, "Go ahead. I'm watching."
The man tees off.  Then he asks Marty, "Did you see where the ball went?"

Marty says, "Of course I saw it."
The man asks, "Great! Where did it go?"

Marty says, "I forgot."

– Norman Tischler

27) One day in an elementary school in Ann Arbor, Michigan, a teacher asks her class if the Michigan Wolverines are their favorite football team. The whole class says "yes" except for Little Jimmy.

The teacher asks, "What's your favorite football team, Jimmy?"

Little Jimmy says, "The Ohio State Buckeyes."

The teacher asks, "Well, why is that?"

Little Jimmy says, "Well, my dad is a Buckeye fan, my mom is a Buckeye fan, so I guess that makes me a Buckeye fan."

The teacher, angered by his reply says, "If your dad was a moron and your mom was an idiot what would that make you?"

Little Jimmy says, "Well, I guess that would make me a Michigan fan."

– Marjorie J. Preston

28) One foggy night, a Buckeye fan was heading north from Columbus and a Michigan fan was driving south from Ann Arbor. While crossing a narrow bridge, they hit each other head-on, mangling both cars.

The Michigan fan manages to climb out of his car and survey the damage. He looks at his twisted car and says, "Man, I'm lucky to be alive!"

Likewise, the Buckeye fan gets out of his car uninjured, he too feeling fortunate to have survived.

The Wolverine fan walks over to the Buckeye fan and says, "Hey, man, I think this is a sign that we should put away our petty differences and live as friends instead of being rivals."

The Buckeye fan thinks for a moment and says, "You know, you're absolutely right! We should be friends. In fact, I'm going to see if something else survived the wreck."

The Buckeye fan then pops open his trunk and removes a full, undamaged bottle of Jack Daniel's. He says to the Wolverine, "I think this is another sign--we should toast to our newfound friendship."

The Wolverine fan agrees and grabs the bottle. After sucking down half of the bottle, the Wolverine fan hands it back to the Buckeye fan and says, "Your turn!"

The Buckeye fan calmly twists the cap back on the bottle, throws the rest of the bottle over the bridge into the river and says, "Nah, I think I'll just wait for the cops to show up."

– Marjorie J. Preston

29) Q. What did the Michigan graduate say to the Ohio State graduate?

A. "Welcome to McDonald's. May I take your order, please?"

– Marjorie J. Preston

30) Four college alumni were climbing a mountain one day: an Ohio State grad, a Michigan grad, a Penn State grad, and a Notre Dame grad. Each proclaimed to be the most loyal of all fans at their alma mater.

As they climbed higher, they argued as to which one of them was the most loyal of all. They continued to argue all the way up the mountain, and finally as they reached the top, the Notre Dame grad hurled himself off the mountain, shouting "This is for the Fighting Irish!" as he fell to his doom.

Not wanting to be outdone, the Penn State grad threw himself off the mountain proclaiming, "This is for the Nittany Lions!"

Seeing this the OSU grad walked over and shouted, "This is for the Buckeyes!" and pushed the Wolverine off the side of the mountain.

– Marjorie J. Preston

31) Q: How do you keep the Cleveland Browns out of your front yard?

A: Install a goalpost in it.

– Mark Mazzocco

32) Q: Why are there so many unsolved murders in southern Ohio?

A: Because all the DNA is the same and there are no dental records.

– Mark Mazzocco

33) An announcement comes over a grade school PA system: "Mrs. Waters, please report to the security office. We have found your eleven children and they are currently beating the Browns 17-0."

– Michael Sonby

34) Q: Where does a Clevelander store their leftover potato pierogies?

A: In the refrigertater.

– Melissa Logsdon

35) Q: Why is Ohio shaped like a heart?

A: Because we want you to love us.

– Graham Kristensen

36) Why couldn't the Baby Jesus be born in New Concord, Ohio? Because they couldn't find three wise men and a virgin.

– Tyler Alexander Morrison

37) Q: What do you call a Cleveland Brown with a Super Bowl ring?

A: A thief!

– Jim Herchek

38) Q: What's the difference between Cleveland and the Titanic?

A: Cleveland has a better orchestra.

– Jerome Masek

39) "Bowling Green, Ohio is so flat…"

"How flat is it?"

"It's so flat that when the wind whips through town, the locals call it 'Blowing Green'."

– Marjorie J. Preston

40) "Bowling Green, Ohio gets so hot in the summer..."

"How hot does it get?"

"It's so hot, the locals call it 'Boiling Groin'."

– Marjorie J. Preston

41) Q: Why were they covering the Ohio Stadium field with toilet paper?

A: Because pollsters say that the Buckeyes look better on paper!

– Marjorie J. Preston

42) I heard there was once a war between Michigan and
Ohio over Toledo. Ohio lost.

– Brenda Fite

43) Q: Do you know why there are so many hillbillies in the Canton/Akron area?

A: They ran out of gas before reaching Cleveland.

– Mark Rapp

44) A label and tag salesman is calling his list of customers in Bowling Green, Ohio, and upon reaching one number, instead of getting who he expected to get, he hears a young voice who quickly and quietly says, "Hello."

The salesman says, "Hello, who am I talking to?"

A young boy's voice replies, "This is Jimmy."

"Hello, Jimmy," says the salesman. "How old are you?"

"I'm six," Jimmy replies.

"Is your father there?" asks the salesman.

"No, he's busy," Jimmy replies.

"Is your mother around?" asks the salesman.

"No, she's busy too," says Jimmy.

"Is there any adult I could talk to?" asks the salesman.

"Well, the police are here," Jimmy says.

"Can I talk to them?" asks the persistent salesman.

"Well, they're busy," says Jimmy.

"Is there anyone else there?" asks the salesman.

"Well, the firefighters are here, too, but they're busy too.

The salesman asks, "What's going on?"

Jimmy replies, "Well, they're all looking for me."

– Jerry Milnor

45) An Ohioan's definition of a buckeye: either an Ohioan or an Ohio State fan.
A Michigander's definition of a buckeye: a hairless nut of no commercial value.

– Marjorie J. Preston

46) OSU and University of Michigan decided to settle their differences with an ice fishing contest. Neutral ground was required, so OSU proposed the Upper Peninsula and U of M agreed. A pond was selected, with each team taking one end. By the end of the first half, the Buckeyes had a great pile of fish and the Wolverines had nothing. Amid accusations of cheating and trading fish for tattoos, it was agreed the teams would switch ends of the pond for the second half. Arriving at the Buckeyes' former fishing camp, the Wolverines were aghast. "Those cheating so-and-so's," exclaimed the team captain. "They were cutting HOLES in the ice!"

– Don Lee

47) A mega-farm owner, trying to impress the third-generation owner of a Western Ohio family farm, thought to boast about the size of his company's holdings. "I can get in this pickup truck right now, step on the gas and maybe reach the other end of my property by sundown," he said. "Yeah, that's rough," said the family farmer. "I had a bad truck like that once."

– Don Lee

48) A guy took his blonde girlfriend to her first Bengals football game. They had great seats near the field. After the game, he asked her how she liked it. "Oh, I really liked it," she replied, "especially the tight pants and all the big muscles, but I just couldn't understand why they were killing each other over 25 cents." Dumbfounded, her boyfriend asked, "What do you mean?"

"Well, they flipped a coin, one team got it and then for the rest of the game, all they kept screaming was... 'Get the quarterback! Get the quarterback'! I'm like...Helloooooo? It's only 25 cents!"

– Marjorie J. Preston

49) In Kentucky, the three Rs are Readin', Writin', and Route 23 to Columbus.

– Don Milnor

50) A dumb Ohioan moved to West Virginia, and raised the average IQ of both states.

– Don Milnor

51) Victoria's Secret?  She's not from Ohio, but she lives there now. (Victoria's Secret is headquartered in Columbus.)

– Marjorie J. Preston

52) Q: What do they hand out at Kentucky graduation ceremonies?

A: A diploma and a map of Ohio.

– Mark Winslow

53) A young BGSU grad was pulled over by an Ohio State Trooper. The state trooper asked: "Do you have any ID?" To which the young BGSU grad responded: "About what?"

– Victor L. Parisian

54) A recent University of Toledo grad was pulled over for speeding by an Ohio State Trooper.
As the State Trooper walked to her car window, flipping open his ticket book, she said, "I bet you are going to sell me a ticket to the Ohio State Trooper Ball."
He replied, "Ohio State Troopers don't have balls."
There was a moment of silence while she smiled, and he realized what he'd just said. He then closed his book, got back in his patrol car and left. She was laughing too hard to start her car.

– Victor L. Parisian

55) A man enrolled in the first math P.h.D. program offered at BGSU back in the 1970s, and on his first day at BGSU, he asked his professor what he should know about a career in Mathematics. The professor replied, "Well, your first math lesson is that P.h.D. stands for "Probably heavily in Debt."

– Maryanne Spielman and Marjorie J. Preston

56) Q: Why do half the students enrolled in Intro to Geometry at University of Cincinnati drop out the first week?

A: They find out they will not be learning about "pie."

– Marjorie J. Preston

57) Q: What did the young mathematician at BGSU present to his fiancée when he wanted to propose?

A: A polynomial ring!

– Jeff Spielman

58) Q: Why did the professors at BGSU never serve beer at a math party?

A: Because you can't drink and derive.

– Maryann Spielman

59) Q: Why are so many astronauts from Ohio?

A: They just want to escape the political ads!

– Marjorie J. Preston

60) A young man from Youngstown is hosting his cousin from Cleveland for the weekend. As they are driving around Youngstown, the Youngstown resident blasts through a red light.

The Clevelander yells, "Hey, cuz!  Look, out!  You didn't even stop at that red light."

The Youngstown resident says, "Oh, believe me – it's scarier when you stop."

– Marjorie J. Preston

61) A little boy in Youngstown hears the phrase "cell phone" and asks his teacher what it is. His teacher encouragingly says, "Well, Johnny, what do you think it is?"
Johnny replies, "Is it that telephone I used to talk with Uncle Guido through that plate glass window?"

– Marjorie J. Preston

62) If your local ice cream shop is closed from September through May, you may live in Ohio.

63) If you've worn shorts and a jacket at the same time, you may live in Ohio.

64) If you've had a long telephone conversation with someone who dialed a wrong number, you may live in Ohio.

65) If "vacation" means going anywhere south of Dayton – particularly if it's North or South Carolina – you may live in Ohio.

66) If you measure distance in minutes and not miles, you may live in Ohio.

67) If you know people who have hit a deer more than once, you may live in Ohio.

68) If you have switched from heat to A/C and back again in the same day, you may live in Ohio.

69) If you can drive 75 mph in drifting snow without flinching, you may live in Ohio.

70) If you install security lights on your house and garage but still leave your doors unlocked, you may live in Ohio.

71) If you carry jumper cables in your car AND know how to use them, you may live in Ohio.

72) If your kid's costume is designed to fit over a snowsuit, you may live in Ohio.

73) If driving in the winter is better because the potholes are filled with snow, you may live in Ohio.

74) If you have more miles on your snow blower than your car, you may live in Ohio.

75) If you find 10 degrees "a little chilly," you may live in Ohio.

76) If "vacation" means going to King's Island, Cedar Point or Kalahari, you may live in Ohio.

77) If bands come to your town ten years after they were popular, you may live in Ohio.

78) If you end sentences with unnecessary prepositions, such as "Where's my coat at?" or "If you go to the mall, I wanna go with," you may live in Ohio.

79) If you make words possessive when they are not, such as calling Kroger, the grocery store, "Kroger's," you may live in Ohio.

80) If all the festivals in your state are named for fruits, vegetables and grains, you may live in Ohio.

81) If you know what "cow tipping" or "possum kicking" is, you may live in Ohio.

82) If your local paper covers all national and international headlines in one page and requires six pages for sports, you may live in Ohio.

83) If you know which leaves make good toilet paper, you may live in Ohio.

84) If you know what a real buckeye is and have a recipe for chocolate ones, you may live in Ohio.

85) If you can spell Cuyahoga, Tuscarawas or Wapakoneta, or pronounce Bellefontaine, Scioto or Olentangy, you may live in Ohio.

86) If you know how to spell "C-I-N, C-I-N, N-A-T-I,", you may live in Ohio.

87) If you get stuck behind a bad driver and check to see if the plates are from Michigan, you may live in Ohio.

88) If your first thought isn't Florida when someone mentions Miami, you may live in Ohio.

89) If you think professional football teams are supposed to wear orange, you may live in Ohio.

90) If you live fewer than thirty miles from a college or university, you may live in Ohio.

91) If you know what game is being played when the Mud Hens take on the Clippers, you may live in Ohio.

92) If you know what "pop" is, you may live in Ohio.

93) If you can name a Michael Stanley Band song, you may live in Ohio.

.

94) If you call a bell pepper a mango, you may live in Ohio.

95) If you know what "The Jake" was, you may live in Ohio.

96) Two retired LTV Steel workers from Cleveland are killed in an RTA accident and wind up being taken to Hell until their paperwork can be sorted out in Heaven. Determined to torture them while he can, Satan puts the Clevelanders to work in the sulfur pits, hauling cauldrons of lava from place to place.

Coming back from lunch, Satan is astounded to see the two men laughing and joking with eachother casually while they work. Enraged, he asks them how they can be so happy.

"We're from Cleveland, and we worked at LTV for years. This heat is nothing compared to working there on a humid day in July," one man replies.

"Yeah, and the stench is nothing compared to walking through the Flats," his buddy adds.

Satan growls at them and casts a spell that instantly turns the room into a frozen tundra, hoping that freezing them out might be a better strategy. But instead of shivering, the two men start high-fiving each other and jumping up and down in excitement.

They both start running over to hug Satan, playfully spraying him with tufts of snow.

"Why are you so happy?" Satan demands.

"Hell just froze over! That means the Browns won the Superbowl!"

– Kevin Cleary

97) Q: What's a Michigander's definition of an Ohio trophy wife?

A: A soccer mom with all her teeth.

– Elizabeth Takacs

98) A Floridian and an Ohioan are talking about the weather.

The Floridian says, "Say what you want about the South, but y'all never heard of nobody retiring and moving North."

The Ohioan replies, "Say what you want about Ohio winters, but at least when I return to my house, it's still standing."

– Marjorie J. Preston

99) A blackjack dealer at Cleveland's JACK Casino and a player with a thirteen count in his hand are arguing about whether or not it is appropriate to tip the dealer.

The player says, "When I get bad cards, it's not the dealer's fault. And when I get good cards, the dealer had nothing to do with it so, why should I tip him?"

The dealer says, "When you eat out, do you tip the waiter?"

"Yes," the man replies.

"He serves you food and I'm serving you cards, so you should tip me," says the dealer.

"Okay, but, the waiter gives me what I ask for," says the man. "I'll take an eight!"

– Marjorie J. Preston

100) A man is hitchhiking on the Cleveland Memorial Shoreway on a dark, stormy night. The night passes slowly and no cars come by and the man is getting soaked. The storm is so strong he can barely see a few feet ahead of him. Suddenly he sees a car slowly looming, ghostlike, out of the gloom. It creeps toward him and stops. Wet and cold, the man gets into the car and closes the door. Immediately, he realizes that there is nobody behind the wheel, but before he can react, the car slowly starts moving again.

The man is terrified, too scared to think of jumping out and running. He sees that the car is slowly approaching Dead Man's Curve. He starts to pray, begging for his life, sure the ghost car will go off the road and he will surely die when, just before the curve, a hand appears through the window and turns the steering wheel, guiding the car safely around the bend. Paralyzed with terror, he watches the hand reappear every time they reach a curve. Finally, he gathers his wits and leaps from the car, and runs into town.

Wet and in shock, he goes to a bar and, voice quavering, orders two shots of tequila, and tells everybody about his horrible, supernatural experience. A silence envelops everyone when they realize the guy is apparently sane and not drunk.

About half an hour later two guys walk into the same bar. One says to the other, "Look Scott, that's the idiot who rode in our car when we were pushing it."

– Marjorie J. Preston

101) Q: What is LeBron James' favorite kind of circus?

A: A three-ring circus!

– Marjorie J. Preston